To Joyce
Happy Birthday, _____ happy
cooking in Chinese food.
With lots of _____
Mom & Dad. 1975

THE CHINESE

PARTY COOKBOOK

by

Constance D. Chang

Doubleday & Company, Inc.
Garden City, New York
1973

ISBN: 0-385 01295-0
Library of Congress Catalogue Card Number 72-93463
Copyright ©1972 by Shufunotomo Co., Ltd.
Drawings by Minoru Tsushima
Printed in Japan

THE CHINESE PARTY COOKBOOK

Perhaps you have come across my previous cookbook, THE CHINESE MENU COOKBOOK and perhaps you have tried some of its easy and effective recipes. After the glow of the satisfying results, haven't you wished to show off your newly acquired ability to your friends and kin and share with them the pleasure of delicious Chinese food you have prepared all by yourself?

"Phase II" in cooking is to cook for guests. It is a lot more fun to cook for others—friends, colleagues in the office, relatives, or visitors from faraway places —than just for yourself. And at first, it is a tremendous challenge. This cookbook offers you many special suggestions for home parties, Chinese style, everything from light snacks to full dinners, and for all different occasions. It is hoped that you will find in it the courage and the confidence to prepare Chinese food for guests.

The Chinese people are well-known, indeed, for their hospitality. And everyone is obliged to give a party for some reason, at one time or another, and many people simply enjoy entertaining. To entertain at a restaurant is too common and could be very expensive. Avoid such unnecessary expenses in "Phase II". It's for sure that if you entertain at home with your own cooking, the party will be long remembered and more sincerely enjoyed by your guests.

Family Meals and Banquets.

When invited by a Chinese friend to his home for a meal, you can tell which kind of Chinese meal you will have by looking at the table. If the dishes to be served are all on the table, it is a family meal. The family meal will consist of at least the four basic dishes: one meat, one fish, one vegetable and one soup. You will sit down to a table setting of a bowl of rice, a pair of chopsticks, a soup bowl with a china spoon, and a plate to place your food on. You help yourself to the central dishes. At the end of the meal, hot tea will be served. Fruit or dessert may be served after the meal, but don't count on it.

If you are invited to a banquet, you should also notice the table: a banquet table must be round and is always set for ten to twelve. If more people are invited, more tables will be set. The seat farthest inside the room facing the entrance is for the guest of honor. The seats opposite the guest of honor are for the host and hostess. At a banquet, the different dishes are served one at a time. Appetizers are first, followed by sautéed or fried dishes, then the main courses (about four to six dishes) are served. Soup and dessert may be served between the other dishes as well as as the last dish. Of course, each time the soup and dessert are served, they are of different kinds.

To begin the banquet, the host drinks a toast to the guest of honor, and then the guest of honor expresses his thanks in a toast. The host then helps the guest of honor to the food. Only when the guest of honor starts to eat can the others start. So whether you are partaking of a family meal in the home of a Chinese friend or attending a banquet Chinese-style, you will always feel at home.

CONTENTS

AFTERNOON TEA PARTY

Serves 6

下午茶

I
Eight-treasure Steamed Rice Pudding, Watermelon Basket, Green Tea

(1) Eight-treasure Steamed Rice Pudding

八寶飯

Ingredients:

  2 cups sweet rice or glutinous rice
  2 cups cold water
  Dried fruits such as pitted dates, plums, orange peel,
  red or green cherries and raisins, all cut into small
  pieces as shown in photo.
  4 tablespoons sugar
  4 tablespoons vegetable shortening
  2 tablespoons raisins

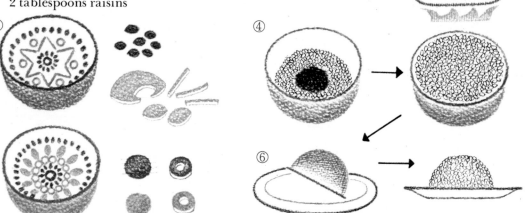

Method:

1. Soak rice for 30 minutes before cooking.
2. Cook rice in cold water over high heat until boiling. Turn heat to low. Cook for 25 minutes.
3. Prepare 6 small greased bowls. Place dried fruits in the bottom of each bowl as illustrated.
4. Mix rice with sugar, shortening and 2 tablespoons raisins. Spoon rice mixture into bowl and press with your palm.
5. Place bowl in steamer and steam for 15 to 20 minutes.
6. Place bowl upside down on plate. Rice pudding is ready to serve. You can keep extra in freezer.

(2) *Watermelon Basket*

西瓜花篮

Ingredients:

1 small round or long watermelon
1 tablespoon rum
1 cup canned or fresh pineapple
1 cup canned or fresh peaches
2 bananas
1 cup strawberries
½ cup canned or fresh cherries

Method:

1. Cut watermelon as illustrated.
2. Scoop watermelon into small balls. Make juice from watermelon remaining in basket. Add 1 tablespoon rum to juice.
3. Cut pineapple, peaches and bananas into small pieces. Then mix with strawberries.
4. Mix all fruits and juice, and arrange in basket.

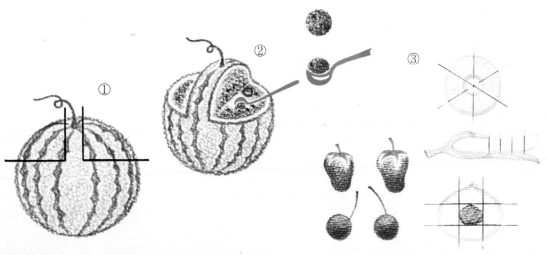

5

II Steamed Cakes and Oolong Tea

Serves 6 to 8

(1) Steamed Brown Sponge Cake

黄糖鬆糕

Ingredients:

2 eggs	⅔ cup sifted flour
⅔ cup light brown sugar	1 teaspoon baking powder
⅓ cup milk	3 tablespoons vegetable oil

Method:

1. Beat eggs well, add brown sugar slowly while beating until thick.   Then pour in milk and mix well.
2. Sift flour and fold into egg mixture.   Set aside for 4 hours.
3. After 4 hours, add baking powder and oil, mix gently and pour into a deep, greased 1½-quart bowl.
4. Bring water in steamer to boil and place bowl in steamer.   Steam for 20 minutes.
5. Cut cake into small pieces and serve warm or cold.

(2) Steamed Prune Cake

枣糕

Ingredients:

30 pitted prunes	1½ teaspoons baking powder
2 cups water	4 tablespoons chopped walnuts
4 tablespoons sugar	few dried red and green cherries
1 cup sifted flour	

Method:

1. Cook prunes in 2 cups of water for 15 minutes.   Set aside until cold.
2. Place cooked prunes and water in blender and mix well, or beat with egg beater until well mixed. To blended prune mixture, add sugar, flour and baking powder, then chopped walnuts and cherries.
3. Pour into greased 7- to 8-inch square or round cake pan for steaming. Steam for 20 to 30 minutes.   Cut into small pieces.   Serve hot or cold.

* You may re-steam these two kinds of cakes after they are cold.

III
Chinese Pastries
and
Coffee

Serves 6 to 8

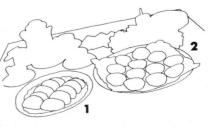

9

(1) Curried Meat Pies

咖喱餃

Makes 1 dozen

Ingredients:

Filling:
2 tablespoons vegetable oil
1 cup ground pork or beef
1 tablespoon sherry
2 tablespoons vegetable oil
1 cup chopped onion

(a) ⎰ ⅔ teaspoon sugar
    1 teaspoon salt
    1 ½ teaspoons curry powder
    ½ slice of bread (crumbled and soaked in 1 tablespoon water)

Pie Pastry:

(b) ⎰ 2 ½ tablespoons lard or shortening
    2 tablespoons sugar
    4 tablespoons hot water
    1½ cups sifted flour

(c) ⎰ 1⅓ cups sifted flour
    4 tablespoons lard or shortening, softened
    2–3 tablespoons water

Method:

1. Heat 2 tablespoons oil in pan, add meat and sherry, cook until meat changes color. Set aside.
2. Heat 2 tablespoons oil in pan, add onion and cook for 2 minutes or until tender. Mix with (a), stir well, add meat and mix well. Set aside until cooled.
3. (b) Mix shortening, sugar and hot water first. Then add sifted flour to make dough.
4. (c) Sift flour into shortening and stir vigorously in a circular motion, drawing dough into ball; add 2 to 3 tablespoons water if mixture will not roll into ball.
5. Roll out first (b) dough into flat circle, about 8 inches across, then place the ball of second dough (c) in the center and wrap in the first dough dumpling fashion.
6. Roll out again into square shape.
7. Roll up into sausage shape and cut into 12 sections.
8. Roll each section into a flat round piece, about 4 inches in diameter. Put about 1 teaspoon of meat in the center of each piece. Fold it into a half-moon, crimping edges as illustrated. (Page 11)
9. Bake in hot oven at 400°F. for 12 to 14 minutes or until light brown.

(2) *Golden Pies*

Makes 1 dozen

Ingredients:

(a) {
5 tablespoons lard or shortening
¼—⅓ cup hot water
¼ teaspoon salt
}

2¾ cups sifted flour

(b) {
3 eggs
1½ cups sugar
1 cup milk
}

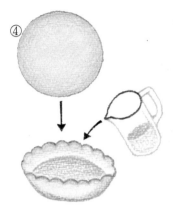

Method:

1. Mix (a) well, then add sifted flour and mix again. Set aside for 30 minutes.
2. Beat eggs of (b) well, then add sugar and milk.
   Remove foam with a piece of paper toweling and set aside.
3. Roll out dough mixture to ⅛ inch thick and cut into 12 round pieces, 3½ inches in diameter. Place each in a separate small tart tin.
4. Place (b) mixture in tart tins and bake in hot oven (400°F.) for about 15 minutes or until custard is set.

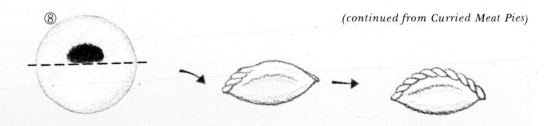

(continued from Curried Meat Pies)

IV Chinese Cookies and Tea
Serves 6 to 8

(1) Laughing Ball Cookies 開口笑
Makes 2½ dozen

Ingredients:

1 ½ tablespoons lard or shortening
1 cup sugar
1 egg, beaten
2 cups sifted flour

2 teaspoons baking powder
¼ cup water
1 cup sesame seeds
4 or 5 cups frying oil

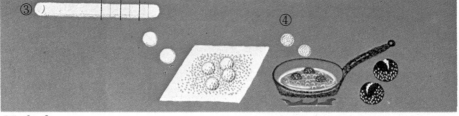

Method:

1. Mix shortening and sugar for 2 minutes, add beaten egg and mix well.
2. Pour sifted flour and baking powder into mixture (1), add ¼ cup of water a little at a time until water is used up and soft dough is formed.
3. Roll dough into the shape of a long sausage and cut it into 30 chunks. Roll gently into balls and dip each one into sesame seeds. (If sesame do not stick to balls, you may use a little water to wet surface.)
4. Heat frying oil to 375°F. Then reduce heat to medium and place half of balls in oil and fry until golden brown. Remove from pan and drain on absorbent paper. Fry remaining balls in the same oil.

(2) Almond Cookies 杏仁酥
Makes 3 dozen

Ingredients:

⅔ cup lard or shortening
1⅔ cups sugar
1 egg
½ teaspoon almond extract
3–3¼ cups sifted flour
2 teaspoons baking powder
1 teaspoon soda
36 almonds

Method:

1. Cream lard and sugar; and add egg and flavoring.
2. Sift flour into egg mixture and blend in.
3. Knead dough till very smooth.
4. Form into 3 dozen small balls.
5. Press an almond into the top of each cooky. Bake in 400°F. oven for 15 minutes.

SNACK AND LUNCHEON

快餐

I
Picnic
Luncheon
Serves 6

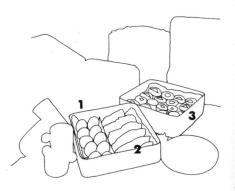

(1) Marble Eggs

茶葉蛋

Ingredients:
- 10 eggs
- 2 ½ cups water
- 3 tea bags
- 3 teaspoons salt
- 3 tablespoons soy sauce
- 1 star anise or ½ teaspoon cinnamon

Method:
1. Cover eggs with cold water and cook for 20 to 30 minutes over high heat.
2. Chill cooked eggs in cold water until cool.
3. Crack egg shells on a table or with the back of a tablespoon without removing shells.
4. Mix 2½ cups of cold water with the remaining ingredients in a saucepan. Add eggs and cook for 50 minutes over low heat. Set aside until eggs are cold.
5. Remove egg shells carefully before serving. Serve with salt or sugar as you prefer.

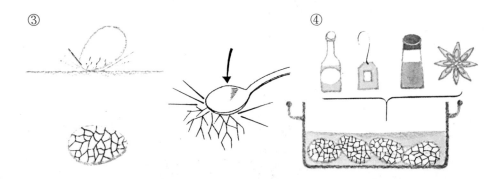

(2) Braised Chicken Wings

Ingredients:

12 chicken wings

(a) {
2 cups water
4 tablespoons soy sauce
1 tablespoon sugar
1 tablespoon sherry

1 Chinese green onion (scallion)

1 small piece of fresh ginger, peeled, or ¼ teaspoon ginger powder

(b) {
1 tablespoon soy sauce
1 tablespoon sugar or a small piece rock candy

Method:

1. Wash chicken wings in running hot water and drain.
2. Mix (a) in saucepan, add chicken wings, onion and ginger. Cook over medium heat for 20 minutes.
3. Remove wings from saucepan. Add (b) to sauce and cook for 2 minutes. Then return wings to pan and cook until sauce is nearly gone. Serve cold.

(3) Picnic Rice-Balls

Ingredients:

5 cups plain hot rice

(a) {
2 tablespoons vinegar
1 teaspoon salt
½ teaspoon monosodium glutamate

1 piece of ham ½ inch thick
1 piece of cheese ½ inch thick
1 small cucumber

Method:

1. Mix rice well with (a).
2. Cut ham, cheese and cucumber into ½-inch cubes.
3. Shape rice into 15 to 16 balls, squares or triangles.
4. Press hole in the center of each rice ball and place ham, cheese or cucumber in hole.

* Rice must be sticky.
  Cook it so that grains will not separate.

1

II Snacks
Serves 6 to 8

(1) Fried Won Ton

炸餛飩

Ingredients:

 1 cup shelled and deveined raw shrimp
 1 tablespoon chopped green onion or scallion
 ¼ teaspoon ginger powder
 (a) { ½ teaspoon salt
    ½ teaspoon cornstarch
    1 tablespoon sesame oil or salad oil
    1 tablespoon sherry
    ¼ teaspoon pepper
 2 dozen won ton wrappers
 3—4 cups frying oil
 1 tomato
 ¼ cucumber

Method:

1. Chop or grind shrimp.
2. Add green onion, ginger powder and (a) to shrimp. Mix well.
3. Wrap won ton as illustrated.
4. Heat oil to 375°F for deep frying. Fry until won ton becomes crisp and brown.
5. Garnish with tomato and cucumber.
6. Serve hot with tomato ketchup or Tabasco.

(2) Egg Rolls

蛋卷

(See page 63)

III Bridge Luncheon
Serves 6

(1) Barbecued Pork or Beef Rolls (steamed or baked) 义燒包

Ingredients:

6 oz. roast pork or beef

(a) {
2 tablespoons soy sauce
2 tablespoons sugar
1 tablespoon vegetable oil
1 tablespoon sesame oil
1 tablespoon cornstarch
}

dough for 20 buttermilk biscuits

Method:

1. Cut roast pork or beef into 1/8 inch cubes.
2. Mix (a) well and cook, stirring briskly, until thickened.   Add meat and mix well again.   Set aside until cold.
3. Make round flat circles using two biscuits for each.
4. Put meat mixture on biscuit circles and pinch shut as illustrated, turn pinched sides down and snip a small x in the top of each roll.
5. Steam in steamer with boiling water or bake in 475° F. oven for 8 minutes.

(2) Corn Soup 粟米湯

Ingredients:

2 cups chicken stock

2 cups canned sweet corn (cream style)

2 eggs

1 tablespoon sherry

1/2 teaspoon salt

1 teaspoon cornstarch (mix with 1 tablespoon of water)

1 tablespoon chopped ham and parsley

Method:

1. Bring chicken stock and sweet corn to boil.   Add beaten eggs and cook for 1 minute.
2. Add sherry, salt and cornstarch mixture.   Stir well and pour into bowl. Garnish with chopped ham and parsley.

IV *Mahjong Luncheon*
Serves 6

(1) Chicken Rolls

Ingredients:

1 cup shredded chicken breast

(a) { 1 teaspoon sherry
salt and pepper
1 tablespoon cornstarch
1 egg white

2 cups vegetable oil
½ cup shredded celery
½ cup shredded bamboo shoots
½ cup shredded carrot

½ cup shredded leek
2 tablespoons oil

(b) { 1 teaspoon Tabasco
½ teaspoon salt
½ teaspoon sugar
1 teaspoon vinegar
1 teaspoon cornstarch
1 tablespoon water

16—18 slices very fresh sandwich bread

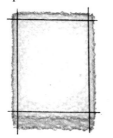

Method:

1. Mix chicken with (a).
2. Heat 2 cups vegetable oil, add chicken mixture.
   Stir for 1 minute.   Remove and drain.
3. Fry shredded celery, bamboo shoots, carrot and leek together in the same pan for 1 minute.   Remove and drain.
4. Heat 2 tablespoons oil in pan. Pour (b) mixture into pan and add chicken and vegetables.   Mix well.
5. Spread chicken mixture on lower third of slices of sandwich bread and roll them like a hot dog.   Wrap in wax paper as illustrated.

(2) *Tomato Juice*

(See page 63)

SMALL ENTER-TAINMENT

各式聚餐

I

Buffet
Chinese Style
Serves 6

Menu
Steamed Chicken (1)
Shrimp with Hot Sauce (2)
Fried Pork Chops (3)
Assorted Cold Noodles (4)
Almond Fruit Float (5)

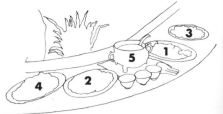

(1) Steamed Chicken

白切鶏

Ingredients:
 4 chicken breasts, skinned and boned
 1 scallion, sliced
 1 small piece fresh ginger, peeled and minced
 2 tablespoons sherry
 1 teaspoon salt
 ¼ teaspoon pepper
 parsley and cherries

Method:
1. Put chicken on plate and add remaining ingredients at once.
2. Place plate in steamer with boiling water and steam for 20 to 25 minutes over high heat.   Set aside until cooled.
3. Cut chicken into bite-size pieces and arrange on serving plate with chicken sauce.
4. Garnish with parsley and cherries.

(2) Shrimp
with
Hot Sauce
干燒蝦仁

Ingredients:

3 cups shelled raw shrimp
2 cups frying oil
1 ½ tablespoons fresh chopped ginger or
   ½ teaspoon ginger powder
1 tablespoon chopped garlic
6 tablespoons chopped scallion

(a) {
1 tablespoon sherry
1 egg white
3 teaspoons cornstarch
}

(b) {
2 teaspoons hot bean sauce or Tabasco
4½ tablespoons tomato ketchup
1 tablespoon soy sauce
1 tablespoon sugar
1½ teaspoons vinegar
½ teaspoon salt
½ cup chicken stock or water
2 tablespoons cornstarch
}

Method:

1. Remove black veins from shrimp. Sprinkle with 1 teaspoon salt first, then wash with water and drain. Mix shrimp with mixture (a).

2. Heat frying oil to 350°F, add shrimp, stirring briskly. Do not overcook. Remove from oil and drain.

3. Heat 3 tablespoons oil in pan. Add ginger, garlic and scallions (If ginger powder is used, reduce oil to 2 tablespoons), stir for ¼ minute. Add mixture (b) and shrimp, stirring constantly until thickened. Remove to serving plate.

27

(3) Fried Pork Chops
炸猪排

Ingredients:
  6 thin pork chops, boned
  pepper
  salt
  ginger powder
  garlic powder
  2 teaspoons oyster sauce or soy sauce
  ½ cup flour
  1 egg
  1½ cups bread crumbs
  ½ cup frying oil
  Tomato, barbecue or plum sauce

Method:
1. Pound meat with steak tenderizer and sprinkle both sides with a dash of pepper, salt, ginger powder and garlic powder.
2. Sprinkle pork chops with oyster sauce and coat chops with flour.
3. Dip chops in beaten egg, then coat them with bread crumbs.
4. Heat frying pan over high heat for 1 minute and pour in a little oil. When oil is heated, turn heat to medium and put chops in. Fry until browned on both sides and pork is cooked through.
5. Cut cooked chops into bite-size pieces and arrange them on hot serving plate. Garnish with tomato wedges and shredded cucumber as shown in photo. Serve with tomato, barbecue or plum sauce.

(4) Assorted Cold Noodles
什錦冷麵

Ingredients:

1 lb. dry Chinese noodles or
   slender spaghetti
salt
2 tablespoons sesame oil or salad oil
1 cucumber
6 thin slices of ham

(a)
  6 tablespoons soy sauce
  1 tablespoon vinegar
  1 teaspoon sugar
  ½ teaspoon monosodium glutamate
  2—3 teaspoons Tabasco

Method:

1. Cook noodles in boiling water for 3 minutes. Rinse with cold water and drain well. Sprinkle with a dash of salt and 2 tablespoons salad oil. Mix well.
2. Cut cucumber and ham into long, thin strips. Mix with cool noodles.
3. Mix ingredients (a) for noodle sauce.
4. Place cool noodles on large plate and pour the sauce over them. Mix again before serving.

(5) Almond Fruit Float
杏仁豆腐

Ingredients:

10 strips agar-agar or
  2 packages unflavoured gelatin
2 ½ cups water
2 tablespoons canned milk
2 tablespoons sugar

1 teaspoon almond extract
1 cup sugar } for syrup
3 cups water
1½ cups canned tangerines
6 cherries

Method:

1. Wash agar-agar. (If using packaged gelatin, soften the powder in ½ cup of water.)
2. Bring 2 ½ cups of water to boil. (If using gelatin use only 2 cups boiling water.) Add agar-agar or gelatin and stir until dissolved.
3. Stir in milk, sugar and almond extract. Strain mixture through cheese-cloth into flat pan about 9 inches square. Cool in refrigerator until firm.
4. Bring sugar and water to boil to make syrup. When cool, chill in refrigerator.
5. Cut almond gelatin into diamond shapes and pour syrup over it. Pour into serving bowl and mix with tangerines and cherries.

31

II
Chinese Pancake Dinner
Serves 6

Menu

(1) Pancake

(2) Chop Suey

(3) Chicken with Green Pepper

(4) Egg with Shrimp

(5) Fried Shredded Potato

(6) Chicken Soup

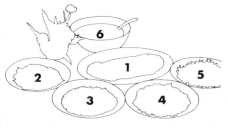

33

(1) Pancakes

薄 餅

Ingredients:

    2 cups sifted flour
    ¾ cup boiling water
    2 tablespoons lard, vegetable
       shortening, sesame oil or salad oil

Method:

1. Mix flour with boiling water. Knead well on unfloured board into soft dough. Cover and set aside for 15 minutes.
2. Roll dough into a sausage shape about 1½ inches in diameter.
3. Cut dough into 12 pieces. Flatten each piece with the palm. Brush salad oil lightly on one side of each piece. Place two pieces together with oiled side inside like a sandwich.
4. Roll out each sandwich into a 6 to 7 inch circle.
5. Bake in flat, ungreased fry pan over low heat for 1 minute and turn over. Bake the other side until slightly browned.
6. Remove from heat and separate each sandwich into two thin pancakes. To re-heat, steam for 10 minutes or wrap in wet cloth and place in micro-wave range for half minute. Serve with other dishes.

(2) Chop Suey

炒 和 菜

Ingredients:

    3 cups bean sprouts, canned or fresh

(a)   1 teaspoon sherry
        ½ tablespoon soy sauce
        ½ teaspoon cornstarch
        ¼ teaspoon pepper

    1 cup shredded lean pork
    3 tablespoons vegetable oil
    3 tablespoons vegetable oil
    1 cup shredded onion

2 cups shredded cabbage

½ cup shredded bamboo shoots

½ cup shredded carrot

½ cup shredded mushroom

12 snow peas (strung and shredded)

(b) {
1 teaspoon salt
1 teaspoon sugar
1 tablespoon soy sauce
}

Method:
1. Clean bean sprouts.
2. Mix (a) with shredded pork.   Heat 3 tablespoons vegetable oil and sauté pork until it changes color.   Remove to plate.
3. Heat 3 tablespoons oil in the same pan and sauté onion, cabbage, bamboo shoots, carrots, mushrooms, snow peas and bean sprouts for 3 minutes.
4. Add (b) seasonings and stir for 1 minute. Mix in pork. Remove to heated plate and serve hot.

(3) Chicken with Green Pepper

青椒雞絲

Ingredients:

1 ½ cups shredded chicken breast

(a) {
⅓ teaspoon salt
¼ teaspoon pepper
1 tablespoon sherry
1 tablespoon cornstarch
1 egg white
}

2 cups vegetable oil

4 tablespoons vegetable oil

⅛ cup shredded scallions or leeks

1½ cups shredded bamboo shoots

1 cup shredded green pepper

(b) {
1 teaspoon salt
½ teaspoon sugar
½ tablespoon vinegar
}

½ cup shredded ham

Method:
1. Mix shredded chicken with (a).
2. To heated pan, add 2 cups of oil and heat to 350°F.
   Stir in chicken and cook until it changes color.   Remove and drain.
3. Heat 4 tablespoons oil in pan.   Sauté shredded scallions, bamboo shoots, and green peppers for 2 minutes.   Add chicken and (b) seasoning.   Mix well.
4. Remove to hot serving plate and garnish with shredded ham.

(4) Egg with Shrimp

蝦仁炒蛋

Ingredients:
4 eggs
(a) { ⅓ teaspoon salt
    1 teaspoon sherry
    ¼ teaspoon monosodium glutamate
1 cup shelled and deveined raw shrimp
(b) { ¼ teaspoon salt
    ¼ teaspoon pepper
    1 teaspoon sherry
    1 teaspoon cornstarch
4 tablespoons vegetable oil

Method:
1. Beat eggs with (a) seasonings.
2. Wash shrimp, drain, and mix with (b) ingredients.
3. Heat 4 tablespoons vegetable oil in pan and sauté shrimp over medium heat for 1 minute.   Add egg mixture to shrimp and fry until set.
4. Remove to heated plate and serve hot.

(5) Fried Shredded Potatoes

炸洋芋絲

Ingredients:
2 potatoes
1 teaspoon salt
4 cups frying oil

Method:
1. Peel and shred potatoes.   Soak in water with 1 teaspoon salt for 10 minutes, drain, and dry with cloth.
2. Heat 4 cups of frying oil to 375°F.   Add shredded potatoes, stir and deep fry until golden brown.   (Be careful to keep potato pieces from sticking together.)

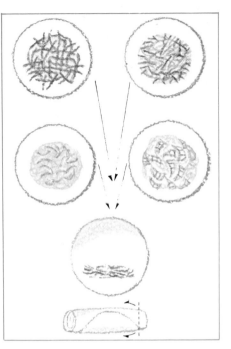

Eating Pancakes

1. *Place the pancake on a plate, and spoon the filling onto the center.*

2. *Roll up as a sausage.*

3. *Fold one end to keep the oil or gravy from dripping.*

4. *Hold the pancake roll using the small finger to support the bottom so the gravy will stay in the roll.*

(6) Chicken Soup

鷄 塊 湯

Ingredients:

2 chicken legs	1 small piece ginger, peeled
6 Chinese mushrooms	1 tablespoon sherry
1 small bamboo shoot	1 ½ teaspoons salt
6 cups water	½ teaspoon monosodium glutamate
1 scallion	

Method:

1. Wash chicken legs in running hot water and cut into bite-size pieces.
2. Soak Chinese mushrooms in ½ cup warm water for 10 minutes and remove stems.
3. Cut bamboo shoot into bite-size pieces.
4. Cook chicken in 6 cups of water over high heat. Add scallion, ginger and sherry. Bring water to boil, skimming off any scum or foam.
5. Add mushrooms and bamboo shoot. Reduce heat to low and simmer chicken soup for 1 hour. Add salt and monosodium glutamate to season. Remove to serving bowl.

III **Chinese Fondue**

Serves 6

Ingredients:

½ lb. beef sirloin
½ lb. fillet of sole
½ lb. chicken breast
    boned and skinned   } Other kinds of meat or fish may be substituted.
½ lb. shelled and
    deveined raw shrimp
    1 leek

few Chinese cabbage leaves
1 onion (shredded)
1 lemon
6 eggs
6 cups water
Seasonings:
    soy sauce, vinegar,
    peanut butter, sugar,
    Tabasco, shredded scallion.

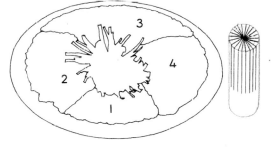

Method:

1. Put beef, sole and chicken in freezer for long enough to firm for easier slicing. Slice into the thinnest possible slices. Also cut shrimp into halves.

2. Cut two 2-inch-lengths of leek stalks. Then cut each down half way from the end as illustrated. Drop them into cold iced water. The cut ends will spread out into flowers.

3. Arrange beef, fish, chicken and shrimp on plate and garnish with leek flowers in the center.

4. Place vegetables and eggs on another plate.

5. Use a fondue set or any other fire pot, or electric saucepan to bring water to boil.

6. Each person selects and cooks his own fish or meat on a fondue fork in hot water.

7. Raw eggs may be broken into individual bowls, stirred lightly, seasoned to taste, and used as a dip for cooked meat or fish.

8. Seasoning may be mixed in individual bowls.

9. Vegetables may be cooked after meat.

10. Lastly, you can also drink broth remaining from the fondue.

IV *Valentine Party*
Serves 4

(1) Tomato Rice with Shrimp

Ingredients:

1 cup shelled raw shrimp	1 teaspoon salt
pepper	4 tablespoons vegetable oil
2 teaspoons sherry	4 cups cold cooked rice
4 eggs	2 tablespoons tomato ketchup
salt	½ teaspoon monosodium glutamate
monosodium glutamate	4 cherries
1 broccoli stalk	2 tablespoons cooked green peas

Method:

1. Remove black veins from shrimp, wash in salted water and drain. Sprinkle with a dash of pepper and 2 teaspoons sherry.
2. Beat eggs, adding a dash of salt and monosodium glutamate.
3. Separate clusters of broccoli and boil in salted water. Drain.
4. Heat oil and sauté shrimp over medium heat for 1 minute. Add beaten eggs and fry until set. Remove from pan.
5. Add cold rice and tomato ketchup. Cook and stir well for 2 minutes. Return egg mixture, add salt and monosodium glutamate. Mix well again, remove to heated plate and arrange into heart shape.
6. Garnish with cooked broccoli and cherries around tomato rice, and form the word "valentine" with green peas.

(2) Heart Shaped Cucumber and Tomato

蕃茄黃瓜

(See page 64)

V
New Year Party
Serves 4 to 6

Menu
(1) Assorted Appetizers
(2) Abalone Soup
(3) Stir-fried Lobster Meat
(4) Stuffed Duck

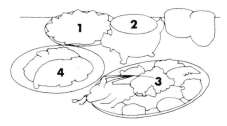

43

(1) Assorted Appetizers
什錦冷盤

Ingredients:

1. Cheese
2. Smoked beef
3. Cucumbers
4. Barbecued pork
5. Abalone (canned)
6. Roast duck
7. Braised mushrooms
8. Ham
9. Steamed chicken breast
10. { Sliced tomatoes   Dip: soy sauce
     Asparagus   vinegar
     Cherries   dry mustard
     Parsley

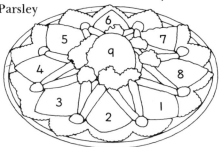

Method:

1. Slice ingredients 1 to 9 into small pieces.
2. Arrange all ingredients as shown in photo. If some ingredients are not available, substitute any other ingredient on hand.
3. Dip into mixture of soy sauce, vinegar, and mustard to eat.

44

(2) Abalone Soup

鮑 片 湯

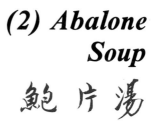

Ingredients:
  5 cups chicken stock
  1 small piece fresh ginger, peeled
  1 scallion
  ½ cup sliced carrot
  ½ cup sliced celery
  ½ cup sliced canned abalone
  ⅓ teaspoon monosodium glutamate
  1 ½ teaspoons salt

Method:
1. Bring stock to boil, add ginger, scallion, carrot, and celery.   Cook for 15 minutes.
2. Add abalone and monosodium glutamate and boil gently for 1 minute. Add salt to taste.   Remove ginger and scallion and pour soup into heated tureen.

(3) Stir-Fried Lobster Meat
炒竜蝦片

Ingredients:

1 live lobster (2—2½ pounds)

12 raw prawns or jumbo shrimps

2 tablespoons oil

salt

2 lb. frozen or fresh spinach

(If frozen spinach is used, see Ham and Spinach
   recipe on page 56 for method.)

2 tablespoons sherry

2 teaspoons cornstarch

1 egg white

3 cups frying oil

⅓ cup sliced onion

½ cup sliced carrot

½ teaspoon salt

tomato, pineapple rings, cucumber and cherries for garnish

Method:

1. Cut lobster into 3 parts. Twist off claws. Remove meat from shell. Slice meat.
2. Shell prawns, remove black veins and slice.
3. Steam head and tail shells of lobster about 20 minutes.
4. Heat 2 tablespoons oil in pan. Add a dash of salt and fry spinach for 2 minutes. Remove to large plate. Arrange steamed lobster head and tail shells on spinach.
5. Mix meat of lobster and prawn together with sherry, cornstarch and egg white.
6. Heat 3 cups of frying oil to 350°F. Pour lobster mixture into oil, stir for 2 minutes until color changes. Remove from pan and drain.
7. Heat 2 tablespoons of the same oil in pan, add onion and carrot. Stir for 2 minutes. Add lobster mixture and salt, mix well. Remove to the middle of plate of spinach as shown in photograph. Garnish with slices of tomato, pineapple rings, cucumber slices and cherries as shown in photo.

(4) Stuffed Duck
八寶鴨

Ingredients:
    4–5 lb. whole duck
    salt and pepper
    4 cups cooked glutinous rice
    ½ cup very finely diced
       lean pork
    1 duck liver (diced)
    3 dried mushrooms (soaked and diced)
    1 bamboo shoot (diced)
    2 tablespoons sherry
    2 tablespoons soy sauce
    1 teaspoon sugar
    5 cups frying oil
    2 cups water
    5 tablespoons soy sauce
    1 scallion and 1 small piece
       fresh ginger, peeled
    2 tablespoons sugar

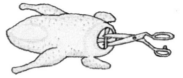

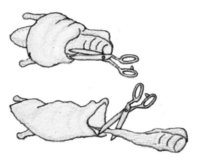

Method:
1. Bone duck as illustrated. Wash outside with hot water and wipe inside with paper towel. Season with salt and pepper.
2. Mix cooked glutinous rice (see page 4) with diced pork, liver, mushrooms, bamboo shoot and 1 tablespoon sherry, 2 tablespoons soy sauce, 1 teaspoon sugar and a dash of salt and pepper.
3. Stuff rice mixture into the cavity of duck and close up opening with clips or trussing pins. Rub duck skin with soy sauce.
4. Heat frying oil to 375°F. in a large deep fat fryer. Deep fry duck until golden brown. Remove and drain.
5. Place fried duck in 2 cups of water. Add remaining 1 tablespoon sherry, 5 tablespoons soy sauce, fresh ginger and scallion. Cook; uncovered, over low heat for ¾ hour. Add sugar and cook another 15 minutes.
6. Cut duck into two or more pieces. Serve hot. Eat duck and rice together.

VI Halloween Party
Serves 4 to 6

(1) Steamed Pumpkin or Acorn Squash

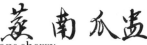

Ingredients:

1 small pumpkin or large acorn squash	⅓ cup diced chicken meat	2 tablespoons sherry
⅓ cup diced bacon	12 shelled and deveined raw shrimp	1 teaspoon salt
⅓ cup diced pork	⅓ cup water	12 snow peas
		⅓ teaspoon monosodium glutamate

Method

1. Cut off top ⅕ of pumpkin to use as a "lid."   Remove seeds.
2. Wash bacon, pork, chicken and shrimp in running hot water.
3. Place bacon, pork, chicken and shrimp in pumpkin with water, sherry and salt.
4. Steam pumpkin in steamer with top on for 20 minutes.   Add snow peas and monosodium glutamate to pumpkin and steam for another 10 minutes.

(2) Stewed Pumpkin

南瓜麵塊

Ingredients:

1 small pumpkin	⅓ teaspoon monosodium glutamate
2 tablespoons dried shrimp	6 cups chicken stock
2 tablespoons sherry	1 cup diced scallion
1 cup sifted flour	½ teaspoon salt
½ cup water	1 tablespoon soy sauce
⅓ teaspoon salt	

Method:

1. Cut pumpkin into bite-size pieces.
2. Soak dried shrimp with 2 tablespoons sherry.
3. Mix sifted flour with water.   Add ⅓ teaspoon salt and ⅓ teaspoon monosodium glutamate.
4. Bring chicken stock to boil, add pumpkin, diced scallion and soaked shrimp.   Cook until pumpkin is soft.
5. Add flour mixture, 1 tablespoon at a time, to boiling pumpkin mixture. Then add ½ teaspoon salt and 1 tablespoon soy sauce.   Cook for 2 minutes.   Serve hot.

COMPANY QUICK

Deep Fried Chicken (1)
Wrapped Beef (2)
Ham and Spinach (3)
Jumbo Omelette (4)
Egg with Crab Meat (5)

Suggestion of Menus

Menu A (Serves 6)
1. Jumbo Omelette
2. Lemon Chicken
3. Salted Green Peppers

COMING!

家常便饭

(6) *Salted Green Peppers*
(7) *Egg and Mushroom Soup*
(8) *Mixed Asparagus with*
   Shrimp and Ham
(9) *Lemon Chicken*

Menu B *(Serves 4 to 6)*
1. **Egg and Mushroom Soup**
2. **Deep Fried Chicken**
3. **Ham and Spinach**

Menu C *(Serves 4 to 6)*
1. **Egg and Mushroom Soup**
2. **Wrapped Beef**
3. **Mixed Asparagus with**
   Shrimp and Ham

4

5

6

(1) Deep Fried Chicken

Serves 4

炸 子 鷄

Ingredients:
- ½ spring chicken
- ¼ teaspoon pepper
- ¼ teaspoon salt
- 2 tablespoons soy sauce
- 1 tablespoon sherry
- ½ cup cornstarch
- 3 cups frying oil
- ½ cup chopped scallions

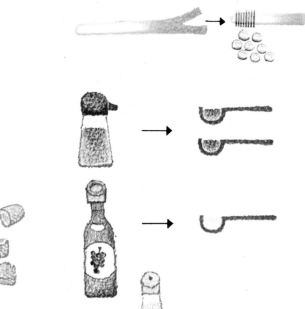

Method:
1. Cut chicken into bite-size pieces, sprinkle with pepper asd salt. Marinate with soy sauce and sherry for 30 minutes.
2. Coat chicken with cornstarch.
3. Heat oil to 350°F., add chicken, fry until golden brown and drain.
4. In dry pan, put scallions and fried chicken, stirring over heat for half a minute. Remove to serving plate.
5. Dip fried chicken into tomato ketchup or spiced salt to eat.

(2) Wrapped Beef

纸包牛肉 *Serves 4 to 6*

Ingredients:

12 thin slices beef (about 2 inches by 1½ inches)

(a)
- 1 teaspoon sesame or vegetable oil
- 1 teaspoon sherry
- 1 tablespoon soy sauce
- ¼ teaspoon ginger powder

12 snow peas
12 (6-inch) squares grease-proof or waxed paper
12 pieces leek or scallion sliced lengthwise (about 2 inches long)
4 cups frying oil
1 tomato
parsley

Method:

1. Marinate beef in (a) mixture for 15 minutes.
2. String snow peas.
3. Rub each sheet of grease-proof paper with a little oil. Place on each of them a slice of beef, a snow pea and a slice of leek. Fold opposite corners of paper, then pinch edges together as illustrated.
4. Heat oil to 375°F. and deep fry wrapped beef 2 to 3 minutes on each side until light brown. Place on plate and garnish with tomato and parsley as shown in photo.

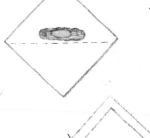

(3) *Ham and Spinach*

Serves 4 to 6

火腿菠菜

Ingredients:
    2 lb. fresh spinach
    4 tablespoons vegetable oil
    ½ teaspoon salt
    5 slices ham
    1 clove garlic
    2 tablespoons vegetable oil
    ⅓ teaspoon salt
    ⅓ teaspoon monosodium glutamate
    ⅓ teaspoon sugar

Method:
1. Cut spinach into 3 to 4 inch lengths, wash and drain.
2. Heat 4 tablespoons oil with ½ teaspoon salt first, then add spinach. Stir while cooking for 2 minutes. Drain off oil. (If frozen spinach is used, omit step (1) and (2). Boil in salted water and drain.)
3. Cut ham into small pieces, slice garlic and set aside.
4. Heat 2 tablespoons oil, add garlic and ham, stir for one minute. Add spinach, salt, monosodium glutamate and sugar. Mix well. Remove to heated plate.

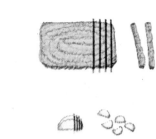

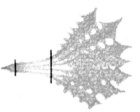

(4) Jumbo Omelette
Serves 4 to 6

爆　　蛋

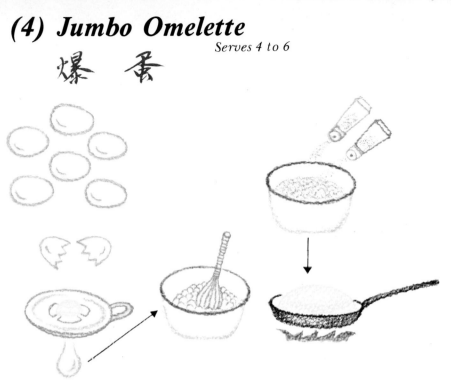

Ingredients:
  6 eggs
  ½ teaspoon salt
  ¼ teaspoon monosodium glutamate
  ¼ cup vegetable oil for frying
  parsley

Method:
1. Separate egg yolks from whites.　Beat egg whites until stiff.
2. Beat egg yolks well while adding ½ teaspoon salt and ¼ teaspoon mono-
    sodium glutamate.
    Blend with egg whites.
3. Heat oil in a large skillet and add egg mixture.　Fry one side until light
    brown, turn over and cook for half a minute.　Then turn over once again.
    Remove to heated serving plate after a few seconds.
    Garnish with parsley.

(5) *Egg with Crab Meat*

Serves 6

芙蓉蟹

Ingredients:

    1 cup crab meat
    6 eggs, beaten
    ⅓ cup water

(a) {
    ⅔ teaspoon salt
    ⅓ teaspoon monosodium glutamate
    ¼ teaspoon ginger powder
    2 teaspoons sherry
}

    6 tablespoons vegetable oil
    ½ cup shredded onion
    ½ cup shredded carrot
    ½ cup shredded cucumber
    4 shredded canned mushrooms

(b) {
    3 tablespoons tomato ketchup
    2 tablespoons vinegar
    2 tablespoons sugar
    ⅓ teaspoon salt
    ¼ teaspoon monsodium glutamate
    ⅓ cup water
    1 tablespoon cornstarch
}

    1 tablespoon vegetable oil

Method:

1.   Remove cartilage from crab meat and flake; mix with beaten eggs, water and (a) mixture.
2.   Heat 2 tablespoons vegetable oil, add onion, carrot, cucumber and mushrooms. Cook for 2 minutes and add to egg mixture.
3.   Heat 4 tablespoons oil, add egg and vegetable mixture and stir until set. Remove to plate.
4.   Cook and stir (b) mixture until thickened. Sprinkle with 1 tablespoon oil. Pour over the eggs.

(6) Salted Green Peppers

醃青椒

Serves 6

Ingredients:
- 3 large green peppers
- 1 teaspoon salt
- 1 tomato
- 1 tablespoon soy sauce
- 1 tablespoon vinegar
- 1 teaspoon sugar
- 1 tablespoon sesame oil
- ⅓ teaspoon monosodium glutamate

Method:
1. Slice green peppers as illustrated, mix with 1 teaspoon salt and let stand for 30 minutes.
2. Slice tomato and arrange on plate.   Add salted and drained green peppers in the center as shown in photo.
3. Mix soy sauce, vinegar, sugar, sesame oil and monosodium glutamate. Pour mixture over peppers before serving.

(7) Egg and Mushroom Soup

蛋花湯

Serves 6

Ingredients:

⅓ cucumber (lengthwise piece about 2 inches long)

5 mushrooms (fresh or canned)

2 eggs

5 cups chicken stock

salt, pepper and monosodium glutamate

Method:

1. Slice cucumber and mushrooms very thin.
2. Beat eggs adding a dash of salt.
3. Bring chicken stock to boil. Add cucumber and mushrooms, and cook for 2 minutes.
4. Pour beaten egg in very fine stream into stock and bring to boil again. Add salt, pepper and monosodium glutamate to taste.

(8) Mixed Asparagus with Shrimp and Ham

拌三鮮

Serves 4 to 6

Ingredients:

1 box frozen asparagus

2 cups water

½ teaspoon salt

{ 4 raw prawns or jumbo shrimp in the shell

2 cups water

½ teaspoon salt

3 thin slices ham

(a) {
⅔ teaspoon salt

1 tablespoon soy sauce

1 teaspoon sesame oil

1 teaspoon sugar

2 tablespoons mayonaise

2 teaspoons vinegar

Method:

1. Boil asparagus in 2 cups of water with ½ teaspoon of salt for 2 minutes. Cut into bite-size pieces.
2. Boil prawns in 2 cups of water with ½ teaspoon salt for 3 minutes, shell devein and slice into small pieces.
3. Cut ham into bite-size pieces, arrange with asparagus and prawns on plate.
4. Mix (a) mixture and pour over ham plate just before serving.

8

9

(9) *Lemon Chicken*

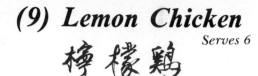

Serves 6

Ingredients:

2 whole chicken breasts, split and boned

(a) { salt
pepper
1 tablespoon sherry

1 lemon (half for lemon juice, half for slices)

(b) { 4 tablespoons cornstarch
4 tablespoons flour

3–4 cups frying oil.

1 large tomato (slice and make a rose shape as shown in photo.)

parsley

4 cups shredded lettuce

2 tablespoons vegetable oil

(c) { 2 tablespoons tomato ketchup
1 tablespoon soy sauce
1 tablespoon sesame or vegetable oil
1 ½ tablespoons vinegar
1 ½ tablespoons sugar

Method:

1. Sprinkle (a) over chicken, then the juice of ½ lemon and marinate for 20 minutes.
2. Mix (b) well and coat chicken with mixture.
3. Heat oil to 350°F. and fry chicken over medium heat until lightly browned. Drain and cut into bite-size pieces. Arrange on plate, garnish with tomato rose, parsley, shredded lettuce and sliced lemon as shown in photo.
4. Heat 2 tablespoons oil, add (c) and cook and stir just until hot. Pour over chicken before serving.

II Snacks

(2) Egg Rolls (continued from page 19)

Ingredients:

(a)
- 2 eggs
- 2 cups milk
- 2 cups sifted flour
- 1 tablespoon oil
- ⅔ teaspoon salt

frying oil
- 1 ½ cups crab meat
- 2 tablespoons chopped green onion
- 1 cup chopped bamboo shoots
- ½ cup chopped Chinese mushrooms

(b)
- 1 tablespoon fresh minced ginger
- ⅓ teaspoon pepper
- 2 tablespoons sherry
- 1 tablespoon soy sauce
- 1 teaspoon sugar
- 1 teaspoon salt
- 1 teaspoon sesame oil
- 2 teaspoons cornstarch

(c)
- 2 tablespoons flour
- 1 tablespoon water

3—4 cups of frying oil

Method:
1. Mix (a) well to make batter.
2. Rub oil on bottom of a small (about 6-inch) frying pan and heat pan for 30 seconds.
3. Pour batter into frying pan, one portion (about 2 tablespoons) at a time to make 16 pancakes.
4. Mix (b) well to make filling.
5. Wrap filling in pancakes as illustrated.
6. Mix (c) to seal pancake rolls.
7. Heat frying oil to 375°F. Deep fry egg rolls until light brown.
8. Garnish with lettuce. Serve hot with tomato ketchup or Tabasco.

IV Mahjong Luncheon

(2) Tomato Juice (continued from page 22)

Ingredients:
- 1 lemon
- 4 cups canned tomato juice
- 1 teaspoon Worcestershire sauce
- ⅓ teaspoon salt
- ¼ teaspoon monosodium glutamate

Method:
1. Slice 4 pieces lemon from the whole one. Make the rest lemon into juice.
2. Mix tomato juice with lemon juice, Worcestershire sauce, salt and monosodium glutamate.
3. Serve the mixture in glasses and garnish with lemon slices as shown in photo.

IV Valentine Party

(2) Heart Shaped Cucumber and Tomato (continued from page 41)

Ingredients:

1 tomato

3 cucumbers

salt

(a) {
1 teaspoon soy sauce
1 tablespoon vinegar
1 tablespoon sesame oil
½ teaspoon salt
½ teaspoon sugar
}

Method:

1. Cut tomato into wedges.
2. Make thin slices ¾ of the way through each cucumber as illustrated.
3. Sprinkle a dash of salt on cucumbers and pull them into long strips. Arrange cucumbers and tomato as shown in photo.
4. Mix (a) in bowl and pour it over cucumbers just before serving.

回回回 About the author:

Madame Constance D. Chang is an authority on Chinese cooking, known for her delicious Chinese food and her recipes for these tasty dishes.

At present, Mrs. Chang has under her direct supervision seven Chinese restaurants in Japan. Peacock Hall is the name given to the four located in the Tokyo, Haneda, Yokohama and Hakata Tokyu Hotels. The other three are called "Madame Chang's Home Kitchen." These serve Chinese snacks and tea and her original Chinese home-style dishes.

Mrs. Chang has the enviable distinction of having initiated the first Chinese buffet restaurants in the world. Only Chinese foods and dishes are served—all you can eat—at a nominal cost.

This intrepid lady has appeared on television cooking programs for more than ten years and has established Chinese cooking schools (three in Tokyo). She has written many books on Chinese cooking. Her cookbooks are illustrated with original drawings, in color, of her dishes which are easy to make and delicious to taste. These attractive cookbooks are a natural outgrowth of the artistry of Mrs. Chang who in her own right is recognized for her Chinese paintings and calligraphy.